Academic & Trade Spring Catalog 2025

Heritage Christian University Press

Cypress Publications

Heritage Christian University Press

PO Box HCU

Florence, AL 35630

ISBN 978-1-956811-84-1 (paperback) ; 978-1-956811-85-8 (ebook)

Contents

About Us

HERITAGE
CHRISTIAN UNIVERSITY
PRESS

Heritage Christian University Press extends the University's mission of advancing churches of Christ by promoting, publishing, and disseminating works of intellectual and cultural significance and enduring value.

Cypress Publications extends the University's mission of advancing churches of Christ by promoting and publishing practical works that will help our students, faculty, and neighboring congregations (broader community) better serve the Lord.

CYPRESS

A Brief History

Although International Bible College occasionally published a few books before its name change, Heritage Christian University Press and its imprint, Cypress Publications, began in 2002 when HCU Vice President Vernon Shuffett penned *As the Waters Cover the Sea: Heritage Christian University: The International Bible College Era.* Shuffett's book remains a noble effort.

In another sense, HCU Press began in 2006 as Heritage Press with the work of alumnus James Farris, publishing *The Great Commission Part II: Becoming the Hands of Christ* by alumni Steve Cummings and Glenn Newton. Dennis Jones, President of HCU, with the consent of the Administrative Council, formally created Heritage Press under the leadership of Lori Eastep (Director of Public Relations) and James Farris in December 2007. Under the guidance of the HCU Public Relations Department, Heritage Press published seven titles through 2017.

Heritage Press began publishing the Berean Study Series annually in 2015 under Dr. Ed Gallagher's editorship. His editorship of this series continued through 2018.

In its current form, Heritage Christian University Press began on January 2, 2019, with the formation of the Heritage Christian University Press Committee. Jamie Cox serves as Executive Director, Brad McKinnon is Managing Editor, and Bill Bagents is Associate Director. The Press offers two imprints: Heritage Christian University Press for more scholarly volumes and Cypress Publications, written for a broader audience among church members. To date, Heritage Christian University Press has published more than 60 books, including its initial Spanish-language volume in 2024. Most titles are available in both print and electronic forms.

The Press anticipates continuing its mission of aiding Biblical studies and encouraging Christian living. Therefore, a 5-year Bible class curriculum template using Heritage Christian University Press titles was first included in the Fall 2024 Academic and Trade Catalog.

Contact Us
press@hcu.edu

Heritage Christian University Press
P.O. Box HCU
Florence, AL 35630

Visit Our Store
Heritage Christian University Press
3625 Helton Drive
Florence, AL 35630

Visit our Website
www.hcu.edu/publications

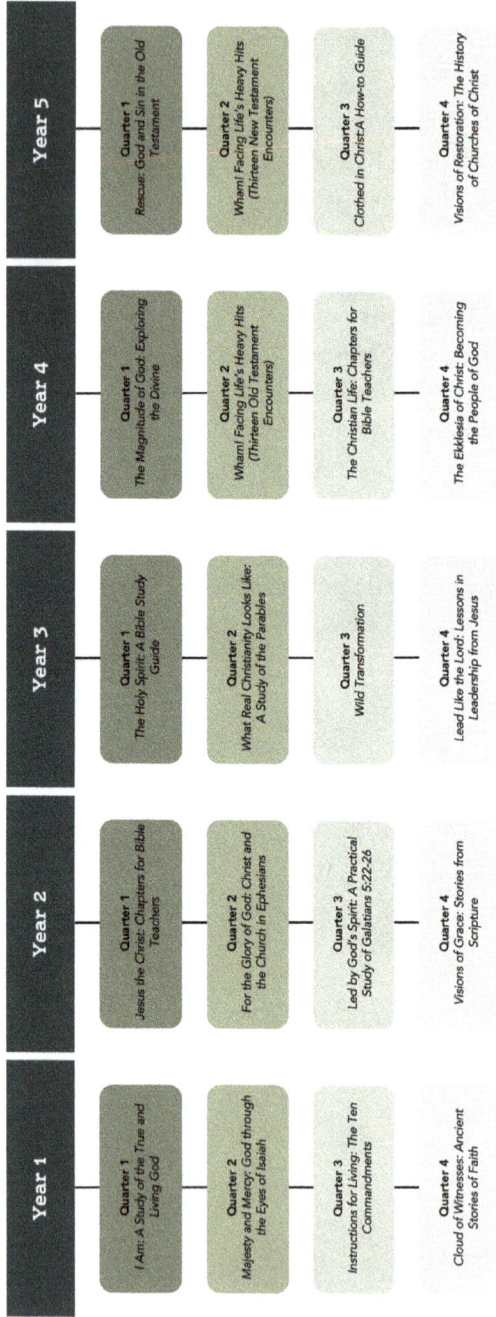

Five-Year Adult Bible Class Curriculum Map

HCU Press/Cypress Publications

Legend:
- Theology
- Biblical Text
- Christian Living
- Special Topics

Year 1

Quarter 1
I Am: A Study of the True and Living God

Quarter 2
Majesty and Mercy: God through the Eyes of Isaiah

Quarter 3
Instructions for Living: The Ten Commandments

Quarter 4
Cloud of Witnesses: Ancient Stories of Faith

Year 2

Quarter 1
Jesus the Christ: Chapters for Bible Teachers

Quarter 2
For the Glory of God: Christ and the Church in Ephesians

Quarter 3
Led by God's Spirit: A Practical Study of Galatians 5:22-26

Quarter 4
Visions of Grace: Stories from Scripture

Year 3

Quarter 1
The Holy Spirit: A Bible Study Guide

Quarter 2
What Real Christianity Looks Like: A Study of the Parables

Quarter 3
Wild Transformation

Quarter 4
Lead Like the Lord: Lessons in Leadership from Jesus

Year 4

Quarter 1
The Magnitude of God: Exploring the Divine

Quarter 2
Wham! Facing Life's Heavy Hits (Thirteen Old Testament Encounters)

Quarter 3
The Christian Life: Chapters for Bible Teachers

Quarter 4
The Ekklesia of Christ: Becoming the People of God

Year 5

Quarter 1
Rescue: God and Sin in the Old Testament

Quarter 2
Wham! Facing Life's Heavy Hits (Thirteen New Testament Encounters)

Quarter 3
Clothed in Christ: A How-to Guide

Quarter 4
Visions of Restoration: The History of Churches of Christ

Berean Study Series

The Berean Study Series is a practical resource guide designed to strengthen your Bible study. Each title presents 12–15 lessons focused on a central theme. The Berean Study Series—an annual written by faculty, staff, and alumni of Heritage Christian University—can be used for Bible classes or individual study. Additional resources for each volume in the series can be found on the HCU YouTube page.

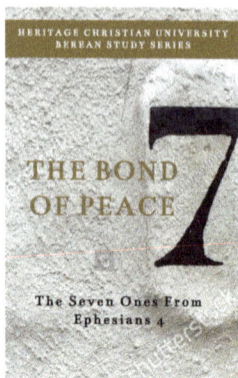

The Bond of Peace: The Seven Ones from Ephesians 4
Coming 2026

1. ONE BODY — Jeremy Barrier
   2. ONE SPIRIT — Ed Gallagher
   3. ONE HOPE — Kirk Brothers
   4. ONE LORD — Michael Jackson
   5. ONE FAITH — Nathan Daily
   6. ONE BAPTISM — Justin Guin
   7. ONE GOD — Andrew Phillips

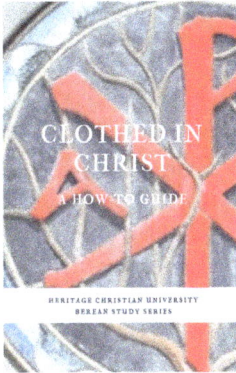

Clothed in Christ: A How-to Guide is designed to help God's people, and especially new Christians, understand some of the important basics of living a Christian life.

Clothed in Christ: A How-to Guide

100 pages (2017)
ISBN: 97817374-75187
Paperback: $9.99
E-book: $6.99

1. BEING SPIRITUAL — Jim Collins
    2. PRAYER — Bill Bagents
    3. LIVING IN SCRIPTURE — Nathan Daily
    4. BEING A SHEEP — Philip Goad
    5. FRUIT OF THE SPIRIT — Ray Reynolds
    6. WORSHIP —Matt Heupel
    7. SPIRITUAL DISCIPLINE — Arvy Dupuy
    8. EVANGELISM — Jeremy Barrier
    9. MENTORING — Brad McKinnon
    10. AUTHORITY — C. Wayne Kilpatrick
    11. DYING TO SIN — Justin Guin
    12. CHURCH INVOLVEMENT — Lucas Suddreth
    13. HAVING REALISTIC EXPECTATIONS — Travis Harmon

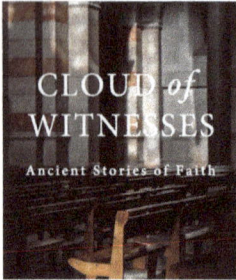

The Bible is full of examples of faith, but perhaps more than any other chapter, Hebrews 11 exemplifies and extols the life of faith. *Cloud of Witness: Ancient Stories of Faith* examines the spiritual role models highlighted in this Hall of Faith roll call, looking for what is exemplary about their lives and how their stories can help us be more faithful.

Cloud of Witness: Ancient Stories of Faith

107 pages (2020)
ISBN: 97817374-66509
Paperback: $9.99 — E-book: $6.99

1. BY FAITH— Ed Gallagher
2. ENOCH— Jeffrey Brothers
3. NOAH— Brad McKinnon
4. ABRAHAM — Michael Jackson
5. SARAH — Justin Guin
6. JOSEPH — Nathan Daily
7. MOSES — C. Wayne Kilpatrick
8. RAHAB — Kirk Brothers
9. BARAK — Arvy Dupuy
10. GIDEON — Philip Goad
11. SAWN IN TWO — Jeremy W. Barrier
12. SAMSON — Travis Harmon
13. SAMUEL — Nathan Guy

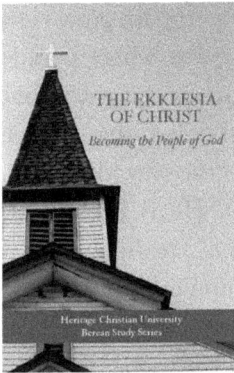

To better understand the Lord and what He expects of His followers, then we need to understand what Scripture teaches about the church—the community of believers He left behind. *The Ekklesia of Christ* will bless you to be salt and light to your community, invigorate you with the message of the kingdom of God, and empower you to fulfill God's mission He has entrusted to His people.

The Ekklesia of Christ: Becoming the People of God

120 pages (2015)
ISBN: 97817320-48324
Paperback: $9.99
E-book: $6.99

INTRODUCTION—WHY THE CHURCH? — Ed Gallagher
1. THE KINGDOM OF GOD — Ed Gallagher
2. THE ISRAEL OF GOD — Nathan Daily
3. THE CHURCH AS SALT AND LIGHT — Bill Bagents
4. FOR ALL ETERNITY — Ted Burleson
5. THE BODY OF CHRIST — Dennis Jones
6. A COMMUNITY OF BELIEVERS — Philip Goad
7. A ROYAL PRIESTHOOD — Wayne Kilpatrick
8. A HOLY NATION — Brad McKinnon
9. CHURCH AND WORSHIP — Jeremy Barrier & Lori Eastep
10. CARE OF WIDOWS AND ORPHANS — Michael Jackson
11. SUCH WERE SOME OF YOU — Rusty Pettus
12. EQUIPPING THE SAINTS — Jim Collins
13. THE MISSION OF THE CHURCH — Travis Harmon

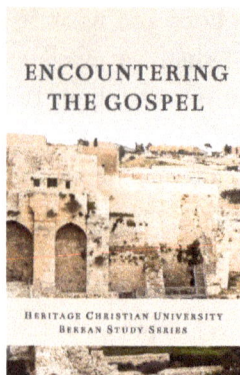

Encountering the Gospel takes the broader view of gospel encounters. Any text where people meet Jesus, hear Jesus, or are taught about Jesus qualifies. Jesus embodied the gospel; Jesus is the gospel. He is "the way, the truth, and the life" (John 14:6). He is both THE question and THE answer. Meeting Jesus is the pivotal point—the moment of greatest significance—in every person's life. *Encountering the Gospel* puts life's greatest decision directly before each of us.

Encountering the Gospel

137 pages (2024)
ISBN: 97819568-11551
Paperback: $9.99
E-book: $7.99

1. THE SYROPHOENICIAN MOTHER — Todd Johnston
2. SHEPHERDS IN THE FIELD — Ismael Berlanga
3. THE PARALYTIC — Andrew Phillips
4. JESUS, SIMON, AND THE SINFUL WOMAN — Justin Guin
5. THE EMMAUS ROAD — Joshua Pappas
6. NICODEMUS — Ed Gallagher
7. THE WOMAN AT THE WELL — Thomas Tidwell
8. THE ADULTERESS — Tim Martin
9. THE MAN BORN BLIND — Thomas Tidwell
10. THOMAS — Zack Martin
11. PENTECOST — Baron Vander Maas
12. THE UNIVERSAL REACH OF CHRISTIANITY—Robert L. Mann
13. THE PHILOSOPHERS OF ATHENS — Jeremy Barrier
14. FELIX — Bill Bagents
15. AGRIPPA — Wayne Kilpatrick

FOR THE
GLORY
OF
GOD
CHRIST AND THE CHURCH
IN EPHESIANS

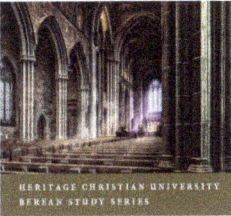

HERITAGE CHRISTIAN UNIVERSITY
BEREAN STUDY SERIES

While suffering in chains, the apostle Paul exulted in the glory of God as revealed in the gospel of freedom. The result was a brief letter to the Ephesian Christians packed with theological weight and practical instruction. *For the Glory of God* includes twelve lessons covering each major section of Ephesians. Each lesson encourages Christians today to take seriously the call of God so that they may grow up in all aspects into Him who is the head, even Christ.

For the Glory of God: Christ and the Church in Ephesians
100 pages (2021)
ISBN: 97810879-39339
Paperback: $9.99
E-book: $6.99

1. IN CHRIST IS EVERY SPIRITUAL BLESSING — C. Wayne Kilpatrick
2. PAUL PRAYS — Travis Harmon
3. LIVING SANCTUARIES —Kirk Brothers
4. THE GREATEST UNSOLVED MYSTERY....SOLVED! — Jeremy W. Barrier
5. PAUL'S PRAYER — Michael Jackson
6. OUR ROLE IN GROWING THE CHURCH — Robert Youngblood
7. TRANSFORMATION IN CHRIST — Jeffrey Brothers
8. FORGIVENESS — Arvy Dupuy
9. FROM DARKNESS TO LIGHT — Clay McFerrin
10. SUBMIT YOURSELVES TO ONE ANOTHER — Nathan Guy
11. MASTERS AND SLAVES — Ed Gallagher
12. BE STRONG IN THE LORD — Justin Guin

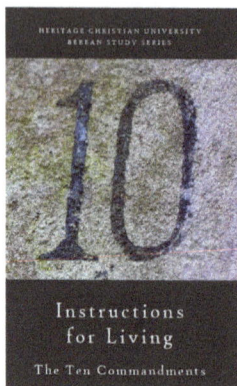

God first reveals His ethical demands to Israel through the Ten Commandments, which serve as the first and foundational summary of God's covenant with His people. These commandments guided the ethical reflections of Jesus, Paul, and James. *Instructions for Living* explores how the Ten Commandments continue to teach Christians about their God and how they ought to love God and their neighbors.

Instructions for Living: The Ten Commandments

119 pages (2018)
ISBN: 9781958-61025
Paperback: $9.99
E-book: $6.99

1. INTRODUCING THE TEN COMMANDMENTS — Ed Gallagher
2. THE CHRISTIAN AND OLD TESTAMENT LAW — Nathan Daily
3. I AM THE LORD YOUR GOD — Jeremy Barrier
4. NO OTHER GODS — W. Kirk Brothers
5. NO IDOLS — Arvy Dupuy
6. THE NAME OF THE LORD — Bill Bagents
7. KEEPING THE SABBATH — C. Wayne Kilpatrick
8. HONORING PARENTS — Philip Goad
9. AGAINST MURDER — Brad McKinnon
10. AGAINST ADULTERY — Michael Jackson
11. AGAINST STEALING — Matt Heupel
12. AGAINST LYING — Travis Harmon
13. AGAINST COVETING — Justin Guin

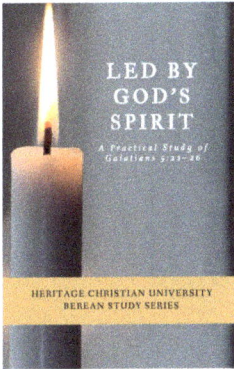

Led by God's Spirit: A Practical Study of Galatians 5:22–26 explores the biblical concept of walking by, being led by, living by, and keeping in step with the Spirit. It features an emphasis on each aspect of the fruit of the Spirit. Each of the fifteen brief chapters includes attention to application and questions for group discussion or further study. *Led by God's Spirit* is intentionally practical, and designed to promote empowered Christian living.

Led by God's Spirit: A Practical Study of Galatians 5:22–26

140 pages (2023)
ISBN: 97819568-11179
Paperback: $9.99
E-book: $6.99

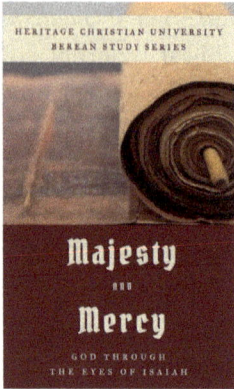

Majesty and Mercy: God Through the Eyes of Isaiah invites us to see what Isaiah saw. Today, God's people remain a light to the nations, comforted, sustained, and empowered by the Father who loves us intensely. With the voice of a prophet and the heart of a poet, Isaiah calls us to lift our eyes in faith so we can see what he saw.

Majesty and Mercy: God Through the Eyes of Isaiah

139 pages (2022)
ISBN: 97819568-11063
Paperback: $9.99
E-book: $6.99

1. THE MOUNTAIN OF THE LORD'S HOUSE — C. Wayne Kilpatrick

2. A VISION OF HOLINESS — W. Kirk Brothers

3. THE COMING KING — Ed Gallagher

4. YHWH IS OUR GOD — Tim Martin

5. GOD'S PEACE — Thomas Tidwell

6. CORNERSTONE AND CROWN OF GLORY — Will Dilbeck

7. THE REIGN OF RIGHTEOUSNESS — Michael Jackson

8. THE HIGHWAY OF HOLINESS — Keith Stanglin

9. GOD'S COMFORT — Bill Bagents

10. BEAUTIFUL FEET — Todd Johnston

11. THE SUFFERING SERVANT — Justin Guin

12. GOD'S HIGHER WAY — Ismael Berlanga

13. GOD'S ANOINTED — Jeremy Barrier

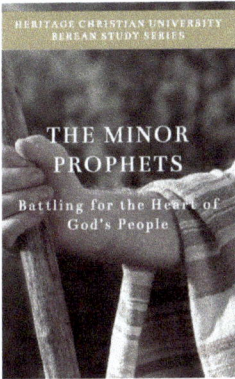

Ancient Israel often lived down to the literal meaning of its name—wrestles with God. They were a most difficult people. And they were not alone in their tendency toward rebellion. Thankfully, God always lives up to His loving and gracious character. Especially through His prophets, God continually fought for the hearts and souls of His chosen people. *The Minor Prophets* powerfully reminds us that He still does. We're blessed to serve a God who loves fiercely, who loves us more fully and more wisely than we could ever love ourselves. To His credit and glory, He makes it stunningly hard to leave Him.

The Minor Prophets: Battling for the Hearts of God's People

150 pages (2025)
ISBN: 97819568-11971 (pbk.)
Paperback: $9.99
E-book: $7.99

1. HOSEA — Justin Guin
    2. JOEL — Ed Gallagher
    3. AMOS — Andrew Phillips
    4. OBADIAH — Clay McFerrin
    5. JONAH — Kaleb Baker
    6. MICAH — Ismael Berlanga
    7. NAHUM — Tim Martin
    8. HABAKKUK — Zack Martin
    9. ZEPHANIAH — Thomas Tidwell
    10. HAGGAI — Baron Vander Maas
    11. ZECHARIAH — Bill Bagents
    12. MALACHI — Todd Johnson
    13. MALACHI — C. Wayne Kilpatrick

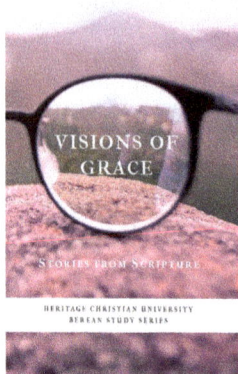

In *Visions of Grace*, thirteen lessons as stories from scripture help illuminate grace, to present a vision of it, or, rather, a series of visions. This study will invite you to live graciously and gratefully in response to His bounteous gifts.

Visions of Grace: Stories from Scripture

135 pages (2019)
ISBN: 97819568-11049
Paperback: $9.99
E-book: $6.99

INTRODUCTION — Ed Gallagher
　1. THE DARKER THE SIN — Bill Bagents
　2. JOSEPH AND HIS BROTHERS — Robin Dunaway
　3. GRACE IN THE EXODUS — C. Wayne Kilpatrick
　4. GRACE IN THE BOOK OF RUTH — Nathan Daily
　5. THE CHALLENGE OF LOVE — Ed Gallagher
　6. A BIG FISH STORY — Travis Harmon
　7. THE GRACE OPPORTUNITY — Todd Johnston
　8. WHEN GRACE APPEARED — W. Kirk Brothers
　9. GRACE IN THE GUTTER — Arvy Dupuy
　10. GRACE IN THE BOOK OF ROMANS — Michael Jackson
　11. GRACE IN THE BOOK OF GALATIANS — Jeremy Barrier
　12. REMEMBERING WHY — Philip Goad
　13. MY GRACE IS SUFFICIENT – Brad McKinnon

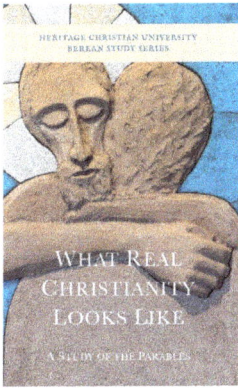

The issue of what real Christianity looks like presses on believers from multiple sides. Is the religion that is spreading around the globe now, the same as what Jesus preached? However difficult the parables of Jesus are to understand, they are much more difficult to put into practice. If we persistently seek the meanings of the parables of Christ, we have assurance that we will find. The 2016 Berean Study Series seeks to find "what real Christianity looks like" according to great stories told by Jesus Himself.

What Real Christianity Looks Like: A Study of the Parables

131 pages (2016)
ISBN: 97817374-75163
Paperback: $9.99
E-book: $6.99

INTRODUCTION — Ed Gallagher
1. ENDLESS POSSIBILITIES — Jeremy Barrier
2. JOY — Bill Bagents
3. COMPASSION — Jim Collins
4. USING YOUR TALENTS — Ed Gallagher
5. MERCY — Arvy Dupuy
6. TAKING RESPONSIBILITY — Philip Goad
7. SERVING — Justin Guin
8. KINDNESS — Travis Harmon
9. LIVING READY — Ted Burleson
10. PERSISTENCE — Matt Heupel
11. HOPE — C. Wayne Kilpatrick
12. INCLUSION — Brad McKinnon
13. GENEROSITY — Lucas Suddreth

Cypress Bible Study Series

The Cypress Bible Study Series by Dr. Ed Gallagher is an annual resource designed to help Bible school teachers prepare quality lessons. Each volume provides background information, links to additional information, and questions to prompt additional study.

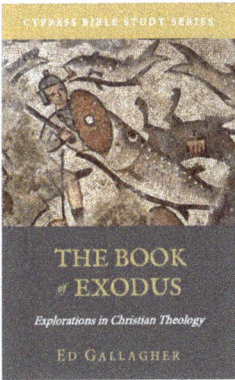

Written for the interested church member, this collection of thirteen studies will push readers to consider more deeply aspects of Scripture usually ignored or lightly treated. Readers will learn not only about the Book of Exodus and its reception in the New Testament, but they will also grow in their understanding of Christian theology.

The Book of Exodus: Explorations in Christian Theology
by Ed Gallagher

348 pages (2019)
ISBN: 97817320-48362
Paperback: $17.99
E-book: $14.99

Designed as a resource for church Bible classes and personal study, *The Sermon on the Mount: Explorations in Christian Practice* carefully considers how Jesus's most famous sermon presents the life of a disciple. Scholar Ed Gallagher argues that the Sermon on the Mount is full of difficult sayings from Jesus that make Christianity squirmy even to discuss, partly because His sayings are not quite difficult enough.

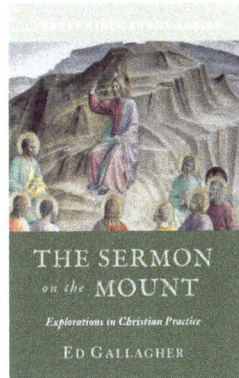

The Sermon on the Mount: Explorations in Christian Practice
by Ed Gallagher
281 pages (2021)
ISBN: 97817347-66547
Paperback: $17.99
E-book: $14.99

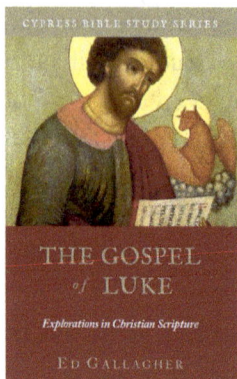

This series of studies on the Gospel of Luke (thirteen chapters with an introduction and a discussion guide) aims to help Christians glean more from the longest of the canonical Gospels. Luke's presentation of Jesus provides important and beloved stories about the Lord, including the lengthiest account of His birth and childhood, a distinctive account of His death and resurrection, and much unique material arising from His teaching, such as the Parable of the Good Samaritan and the Parable of the Prodigal Son.

The Gospel of Luke: Explorations in Christian Scripture
by Ed Gallagher
421 pages (2022) — ISBN: 97819568-11087
Paperback: $24.99 — E-book: $21.99

This study of the book of Daniel in the Old Testament elucidates its theological meaning with a concern for Christian edification. Gallagher situates the book in its ancient Jewish context, considers the history of interpretation, and applies the text to the modern world. Packed with historical information, devotional illustrations, and reflection questions, plus original drawings by Josiah Gallagher illustrating each chapter, this book would work well for personal or small group studies of Daniel's powerful vision of radical faith in a hostile world.

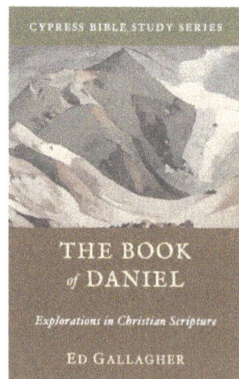

The Book of Daniel: Explorations in Christian Scripture
by Ed Gallagher
221 pages (2024)— ISBN 97819568-11803
Paperback $17.99 — Ebook $14.99

Heritage Christian Leadership Institute Series

The Heritage Christian Leadership Institute Series is a joint effort of the Heritage Christian Leadership Institute and Heritage Christian University Press. This series provides biblically-based resources in support of servant leadership.

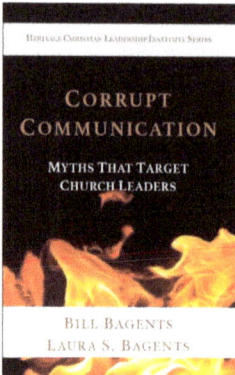

Corrupt Communication: Myths That Target Church Leaders exposes some thirty myths—lies and false messages—that Satan floats to undermine communication within the church. Though ancient, these lines seem ever-fresh. They're crafted for maximum appeal and damage. They always sound right and feel familiar.

Corrupt Communication: Myths The Target Church Leaders

by Bill Bagents and Laura S. Bagents

109 pages (2022)
ISBN: 97817374-75149
Paperback: $14.99
E-book: 9.99

Counseling for Church Leaders offers biblical and practical encouragement to church leaders—in the broadest sense—as they help the hurting. Though Bagents and Snodgrass share insights learned from decades of counseling experience and include resources for further study, their appeal flows primarily from scripture. Their emphasis is on God's leaders helping God's people God's way.

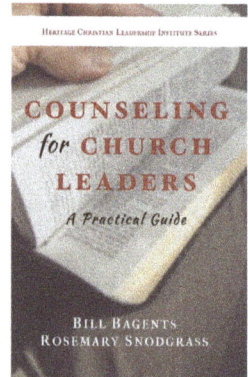

Counseling for Church Leaders: A Practical Guide

by Bill Bagents and Rosemary Snodgrass
316 pages (2021)
ISBN: 97817374-75125
Paperback: $21.99
E-book: $19.99

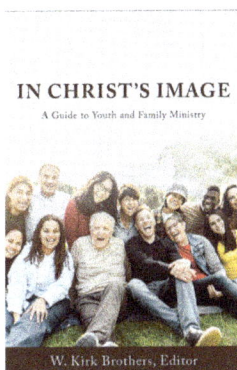

In Christ's Image: A Guide to Youth and Family Ministry is a comprehensive and insightful exploration of the dynamic field of youth ministry. Edited by Dr. Kirk Brothers, President and Professor of Leadership and Ministry at Heritage Christian University.

This extensive volume offers a well-rounded perspective on the multifaceted challenges and opportunities inherent in ministering to young people. Each chapter delves deep into the various aspects of youth ministry, providing readers with a robust and detailed understanding of this vital area of Christian service.

In Christ's Image: A Guide to Youth and Family Ministry
edited by W. Kirk Brothers
694 pages (2024)
ISBN: 97819568-11711
Hardback $59.99
E-book $39.99

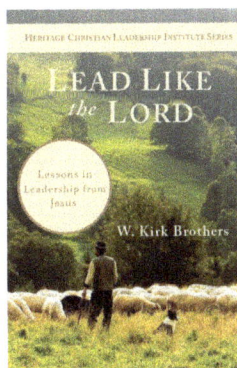

The goal of this book is to challenge us to both live and lead like the Lord. We will be wrestling with what spiritual leadership is and with what leadership success looks like. Along the way, we will focus on nine characteristics of the leadership of Jesus. He was centered, connected, compassionate, common, clear-thinking, competent, courageous, a coach, and a person of moral character.

Lead Like the Lord: Lessons in Leadership from Jesus
by W. Kirk Brothers
244 pages (2021)
ISBN: 97817320-48386 Hardback: $32.99
ISBN: 97819568-11162 Paperback: $14.99 — E-book: $29.99

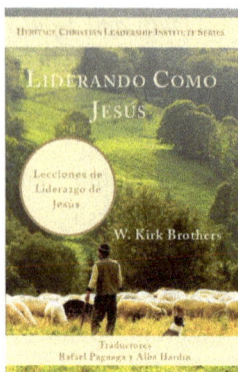

El objetivo de este libro es desafiarnos a vivir y liderar como el Señor. Lucharemos sobre qué es el liderazgo espiritual y cómo se ve el éxito del liderazgo. A lo largo del camino nos cen- traremos en nueve características del liderazgo de Jesús. Era centrado, conectado, compasivo, común, de pensamiento limpio, competente, valiente, un entrenador y una persona de carácter moral.

Liderando Como Jesús: Lecciones de liderazgo de Jesús

by W. Kirk Brothers
198 pages (2024)
ISBN: 97819568-11599 (edición español)
Paperback: $14.99
E-book: $12.99

Heritage Legacy Series

This series follows the longstanding academic tradition of the *Festschrift*, a collection of essays in recognition of a respected colleague. Biblically, it embodies the principles of giving honor to whom honor is due and esteeming godly servants for their work.

HERITAGE
CHRISTIAN UNIVERSITY

Things Most Surely Believed: A Festschrift for C. Wayne Kilpatrick

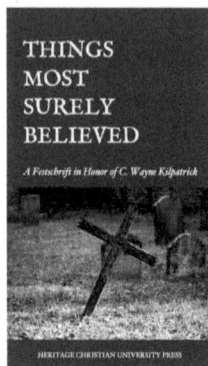

Things Most Surely Believed: A Festschrift for C. Wayne Kilpatrick is the inaugural volume in the Heritage Legacy Series. Personal reflections about Professor Kilpatrick highlight several essays. Topics range from an analysis of Solomon's wisdom to benefactors for abandoned children. The *Festschrift* includes discussions about effective teaching, how God responds to human complaints, and the early development of the journal *Mission*.

218 pages (2021)

ISBN: 97810879-70493
Hardback: $32.99
E-book: $29.99

Serving the Lord: A Festschrift for Freddie Patrick Moon and Janet Stewart Moon

Serving the Lord: A Festschrift for Freddie Patrick Moon and Janet Stewart Moon is the second volume in the Heritage Legacy Series. Chapters include a sermon, reflections on spiritual service, biblical essays, and an excursus on retention in United States Bible colleges. All authors are either former or current coworkers who have been directly blessed by the work of Pat and Janet Moon. *Serving the Lord* reflects the practical service of the Moons as well as their commitment to Christ, His church, and Christian education.

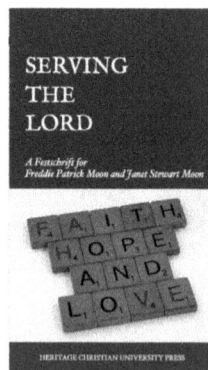

162 pages (2022)
ISBN: 97819568-11100
Hardback: $32.99
E-book: $29.99

Fighting the Good Fight: A Festschrift for Bill Bagents

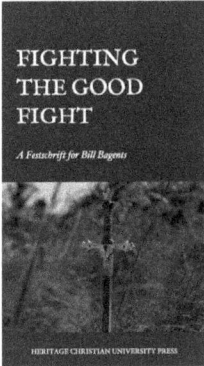

FIGHTING
THE GOOD
FIGHT

A Festschrift for Bill Bagents

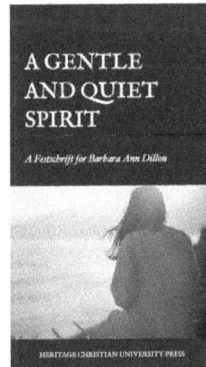

HERITAGE LEGACY SERIES

HERITAGE CHRISTIAN UNIVERSITY PRESS

Fighting the Good Fight: A Festschrift for Bill Bagents is a collection of biblical essays in honor of Dr. Bill Bagents, Professor of Ministry, Counseling, and Biblical Studies at Heritage Christian University. After a heartfelt personal tribute, diverse chapters explore the lament in ancient near eastern literature, four proposals regarding those who "declare the generation" of Jesus, the ongoing meaning of the transfiguration, and more.

236 pages (2022)

ISBN: 97819568-11148
Hardback: $32.99
E-book: $22.99

A Gentle and Quiet Spirit: A Festschrift for Barbara Ann Dillon

A Gentle and Quiet Spirit is a collection of biblical essays in honor of Barbara Ann Dillon, a longtime servant of the kingdom through Heritage Christian University. Rarely does a title of a book so accurately describe the heart of a person.

151 pages (2023)
ISBN: 97819568-11193
Hardback: $32.99
Ebook: $29.99

A GENTLE
AND QUIET
SPIRIT

A Festschrift for Barbara Ann Dillon

HERITAGE LEGACY SERIES

HERITAGE CHRISTIAN UNIVERSITY PRESS

Do All in the Name of the Lord: A Festschrift for Mechelle Thompson

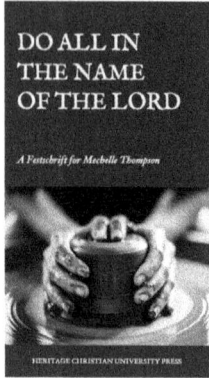

Do All in the Name of the Lord is a series of essays honoring Heritage Christian University's longtime Director of Financial Aid Mechelle Thompson. Chapters include a brief history of Heritage Christian University (formerly International Bible College); calls to kindness, wisdom, spiritual leadership, Christian identity, and maturity in ministry; as well as examinations of Mark 2:23–28 and 7:24–30.

274 pages (2024)

ISBN: 97819568-11490

Hardback: $32.99

E-book: $29.99

John Chisholm Church History Series

In the **John Chisholm Church History Series**, Church Historian C. Wayne Kilpatrick utilizes his over four decades of extensive research of church records, journal articles, unpublished autobiographies, documented papers written for schools and universities, published and unpublished interviews, courthouse records, and even monuments and cemeteries to construct a new history of the origins of Churches of Christ in North Alabama. The first four volumes focus on the four Alabama counties north of the Tennessee River—Jackson, Madison, Limestone, and Lauderdale. This is where the Restoration Movement in Alabama began. Although they faced many struggles and hardships, these pioneering believers were known for their vivid faith as a dedicated band of believers committed to Scripture. This is their story.

A Faithful Band of Workers: The Beginnings of Churches of Christ in Jackson County, Alabama

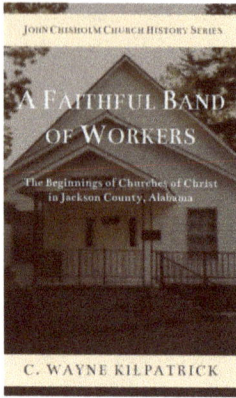

A Faithful Band of Workers considers the beginnings of restoration churches in Jackson County. Attention is paid to the congregations in Rocky Springs, Bridgeport, Stevenson, Scottsboro, and more from the early nineteenth century to the dawn of World War I.

146 pages (2024)
ISBN 97819568-11735
Hardcover $29.99
Ebook $25.99

A Little Band of Disciples: The Beginnings of Churches of Christ in Madison County, Alabama

A Little Band of Disciples considers the beginnings of restoration churches in Madison County. Attention is paid to congregations in New Market, Huntsville, Union Grove, Berea, and more from the early nineteenth century to the dawn of World War I.

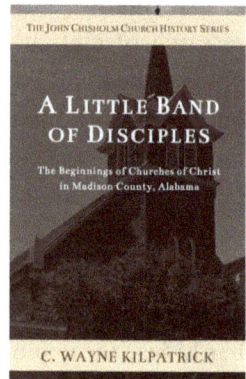

182 pages (2024)
ISBN 97819568-11759
Hardcover $29.99
Ebook $25.99

A Noble Band of Worshipers: The Beginnings of Churches of Christ in Lauderdale County, Alabama

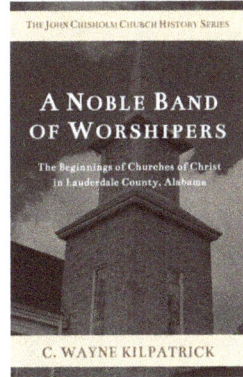

A Noble Band of Worshipers considers the beginnings of restoration churches in Lauderdale County. Attention is paid to congregations in Stoney Point, North Carolina, New Hope, Jacksonburg, Lone Cedar, Pleasant Valley, and more from the early nineteenth century to the dawn of World War I.

　303 pages (2024)
　ISBN 97819568-11797
　Hardcover $34.99
　Ebook $29.99

A Small Band of Brethren: The Beginnings of Churches of Christ in Limestone County, Alabama

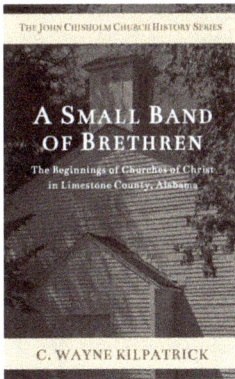

A Small Band of Brethren considers the beginnings of restoration churches in Limestone County. Attention is paid to congregations in Mooresville, Mount Carmel, Athens, Corinth, and more from the early nineteenth century to the dawn of World War I.

　146 pages (2024)
　ISBN 97819568-11773
　Hardcover $29.99
　Ebook $25.99

Onesimus Bible Study Series

The Onesimus Bible Study Series offers biblical lessons for personal or group study from alumni of International Bible College / Heritage Christian University. Each lesson flows from confidence in Scripture as God's inspired, living, and powerful word. Each respects the ongoing relevance of the Bible as it shows us God's heart and guides our service in the name of Jesus. Every lesson is designed to build faith and encourage Christian living.

Why the name Onesimus? We love the brief book of Philemon, in which Onesimus shines as a stunning example of trusting God more than self or circumstance. The runaway slave met the apostle Paul and encountered God's truth. Out of respect for God—and with Paul's blessing and support—Onesimus chose to return to his owner. He did right by obeying the unfortunate and challenging law of the day despite potentially heavy costs and consequences.

Many of our alumni write beautifully. They also exhibit the servant's heart modeled by Onesimus. Their loyalty to God and submission to Scripture model the faithful excellence of Onesimus. We're blessed to know and serve with such fine brethren. We believe they will bless you too.

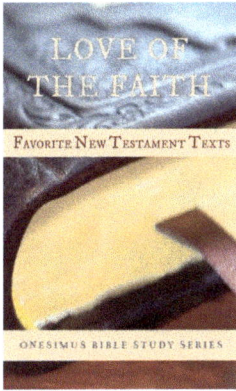

Love of the Faith: Favorite New Testament Texts is the inaugural volume in the Onesimus Bible Study Series from Cypress Publications. It offers eleven chapters from alumni of International Bible College and Heritage Christian University. Readers will find the diversity of styles and expressions refreshing. Those who love the Bible will appreciate the respect for God's word as both relevant and authoritative. *Favorite New Testament Texts* is intended for both individual and group Bible study.

Love of the Faith: Favorite New Testament Texts
by Heritage Christian University Alumni, edited by Bill Bagents
105 pages (2023)
ISBN: 97819568-11476
Paperback: $9.99
E-book: $7.99

1. THE GOD OF RESTORATION — Mike Baker
    2. COOL WATER FOR A THIRSTY SOUL — George Hulett
    3. GOD SHALL WIPE AWAY ALL TEARS — Robert Darby
    4. SHARING OUR BLESSINGS — Jerry R. Self
    5. NEW EXODUS LED BY CHRIST — Jordan Gray
    6. ACCESS — Bryan Collins
    7. NO CONDEMNATION! — Chris Carrillo
    8. FREEDOM THROUGH RESTORATION — Scott Harp
    9. TAKE COURAGE I HAVE CONQUERED THE WORLD — Don Snodgrass
    10. FREEDOM IN THE LORD — Chris Keeton
    11. DID PHILEMON RECONCILE? — Michael Farris

Refreshing the Saints: Favorite Old Testament Texts is the second volume in the Onesimus Bible Study Series from Cypress Publications. Readers will find the diversity of style and expression refreshing. Those who love the Bible will appreciate the respect for God's word as both relevant and authoritative. *Refreshing the Saints: Favorite Old Testament Texts* is intended for both individual and group Bible study.

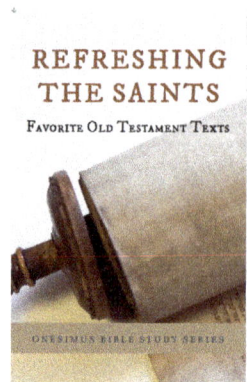

Refreshing the Saints: Favorite Old Testament Texts

by Heritage Christian University Alumni, edited by Bill Bagents
142 pages (2024)
ISBN:978-1-956811-67-4
Paperback: $9.99 — E-book: $7.99

1. THE CREATION ACCOUNT: Genesis 1 — Gary G. Payne
2. WHERE ARE YOU?: An Intimacy Reflecting Question on Your Walk with God: Genesis 3:8–15 — Hong An Tran
3. GO!: Genesis 12:1 — Rickey Collum
4. GOD WILL PROVIDE: Genesis 22:1–19 — Brad McNutt
5. THE LAST WORDS OF SAMSON: Judges 16:23–31 — Dewayne Tapscott
6. PERSEVERING UNDER PRESSURE!: Job 1 — Mark Posey
7. GOD'S FAITHFULNESS: Psalm 89 — Thomas Tidwell
8. PROVERBS 1:1–7 — Lucas Suddreth
9. COME NOW, LET US REASON TOGETHER: Isaiah 1:18 — Walter Rayburn
10. A LASTING PROMISE: Isaiah 43:2–3 — Ralph Richardson
11. ISAIAH 65:17–25 — Baron Vander Maas
12. THE COVENANT OF THE RECHABITES: Jeremiah 35 — Adam Richardson
13. THE HEBREW BOYS: Daniel 3 — James Stephenson
14. YET I WILL REJOICE IN THE LORD: Habakkuk 3 — Joshua Pappas

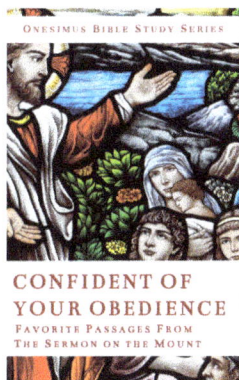

No sermon engages our hearts and minds with more power than The Sermon on the Mount. To this day it stirs both passion and debate. But its goal is far higher; it's a sermon that seeks to transform. It shows us the heart of God, refines our understanding of His truth, and calls us to live God's truth just like Jesus did. Its value can never be exhausted. *Confident of Your Obedience* offers practical reflections on cherished sections of the Lord's most famous sermon from 13 alumni of International Bible College / Heritage Christian University.

Confidence of Your Obedience: Favorite Passages from the Sermon on the Mount

Forthcoming Summer 2025

1. Matthew 5:1–16 — Rusty Pettus
   2. Matthew 5:1–16 — Frank Schapini
   3. Matthew 5:17–20 — Cory Waddell
   4. Matthew 5:21–30 — Don Snodgrass
   5. Matthew 5:31–32 — Eric Waller
   6. Matthew 5:43–48 — Robert L. Mann
   7. Matthew 6:5–14 — Joshua Pappas
   8. Matthew 6:9–13 — Michael Farris
   9. Matthew 6: 16–18 — Russell Wyatt
   10. Matthew 6:19–34 — Travis J. Bookout
   11. Matthew 7:1–5 — Jordan Gray
   12. Matthew 7:6–23 — Baron Vander Maas
   13. Forgiveness — Jeff Johnson

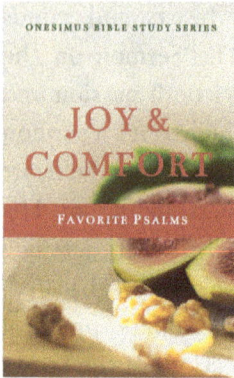

Joy & Comfort: Favorite Psalms

Coming Summer 2026

Radiant Study Series

RAD|ANT

God's warmth in our hearts.   His light in our lives.

The Radiant Study Series flows from a desire to provide quality biblical resources to Christian women. Written by women and for women, it features authors associated with Heritage Christian University. While somewhat patterned after the Berean Study Series, the Radiant series will also include prayer prompts, journal prompts, Scripture-writing prompts, and Bible-marking guides for each topic.

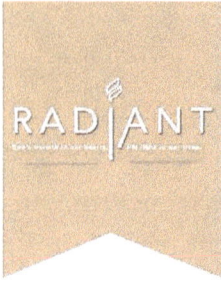

RAD|ANT

our MISSION

Radiant exists for the purpose of cultivating spiritual formation within the hearts of women. We equip women by providing theologically rich resources and opportunities to serve and study scripture.

our VISION

Radiant women look to Him in all areas of life and are transformed into the image of Christ.

Scan to learn more about *Radiant* or visit
www.hcu.edu/resources/church-resources/womens-resources/!

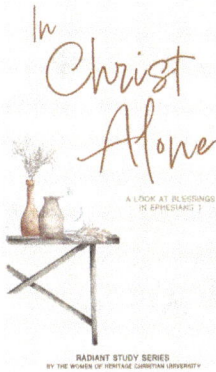

In Christ Alone is a detailed study of Ephesians 1 written by ladies for ladies. The twelve chapters are supplemented by study aids and activities designed to maximize both understanding and application. *In Christ Alone* offers a practical, fresh look at a familiar and impactful text.

In Christ Alone: A Look at Blessings in Ephesians 1

by the Women of Heritage Christian University, edited by Melissa McFerrin and Autumn Richardson

180 pages (2023)

ISBN: 97819568-11391

Paperback: $12.99

E-book: $9.99

Contents

How To Use This Book

Introduction — Autumn Richardson and Melissa McFerrin

1. EVERY SPIRITUAL BLESSING IN CHRIST: Ephesians 1:3 — Debbie Dupuy

2. ADOPTION: Ephesians 1:4–5 — Jodi Gallagher

3. SANCTIFICATION: Ephesians 1:4 — Kim Chalmers

4. GRACE AND FAVOR: Ephesians 1:5–8 — Lori Tays

5. REDEMPTION: Ephesians 1:7 — Teddy Copeland

6. FORGIVENESS: Ephesians 1:7 — Betty Hamblen

7. KNOWLEDGE: Ephesians 1:9, 17 — Cathy Turner

8. INHERITANCE: Ephesians 1:11, 14, 18 — Keli Brothers

9. HOLY SPIRIT: Ephesians 1:13–14 — Rosemary Snodgrass

10. THE HOPE OF HIS CALLING: Ephesians 1:18 — Lori Boyd

11. PRAISE TO HIS GLORY: Ephesians 1:6, 12, 14 — Stacy Harmon

12. THIS IS THE POWER OF CHRIST IN ME: Ephesians 1:19–21 — Jeanne Foust

It has often been said, "A picture is worth a thousand words." However, the opposite can also be true—words can paint pictures of complex and significant concepts, using symbols we can see and identify with to represent things we cannot see but that are very real.

Portraits of God's People invites us on a journey to explore the imagination of God and the beauty of how He expresses who His people are called to be.

Through detailed observations by faithful women of God, the study of these timeless images urges us deeper into our relationship with God and our relationships with one another.

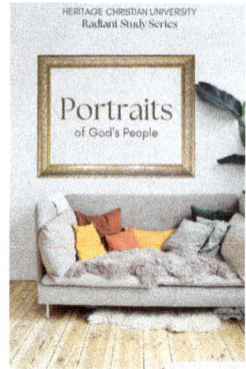

Portraits of God's People

edited by Melissa McFerrin and Autumn Richardson

164 pages (2024)

ISBN 97819568-11698

Paperback: $12.99

E-book: $10.99

Contents

How to Use This Book 1

INTRODUCTION — Ava Johnson

1. THE BRIDE — Lori Boyd

2. THE FAMILY — Jeanne Foust

3. THE BODY — J.J. Davenport

4. GOD'S BUILDING — Melissa McFerrin

5. THE KINGDOM — Autumn Richardson

6. A ROYAL PRIESTHOOD — Carol Sparks

7. BRANCHES ON THE VINE — Molly Daily

8. THE FLOCK — Cayron Mann

CONCLUSION: METAPHORS AND THEIR LIMITATIONS — Jeanne Foust and Autumn Richardson

General Titles

General titles are stand-alone books that support Biblical study and spiritual growth. These volumes offer devotional essays, discuss specific biblical doctrines, explore church history, and offer material for effective Bible classes.

Always Near offers a series of devotional reflections that process events and observations through the wisdom of Scripture. It invites the reader to join the adventure of listening for subtle spiritual messages that both bless and challenge. It promotes contemplation and spiritual formation.

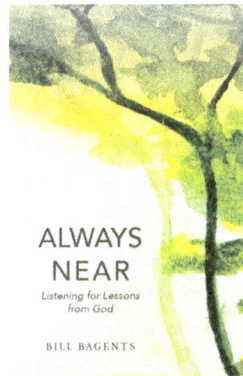

Always Near: Listening for Lessons from God
    by Bill Bagents
    262 pages (2019) ISBN: 97817320-48317
    Paperback: $13.99
    E-book: $11.99

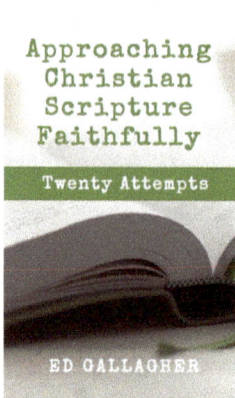

Approaching Christian Scripture offers 20 thought-provoking expositions in four categories: Old Testament Essays, New Testament Essays, Essays on the Church, and Miscellaneous. Though each has been previously published in various contexts, as a unit they model both exegetical skill and faith-building application. Gallagher invites readers to think at a higher level. His loyalty to Scripture is evident. His writing is consistently engaging and challenging.

Approaching Christian Scriptures Faithfully: Twenty Attempts

by Ed Gallagher

274 pages (2023) ISBN: 97819568-11414

Paperback: $14.99

E-book: $12.99

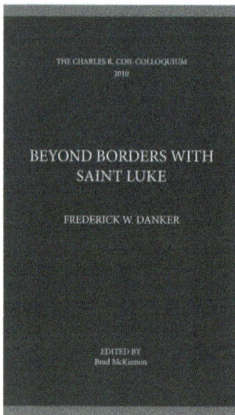

Luke-Acts narrates the God-directed climax in history advanced through Jesus's ministry and in the experiences of the earliest community of Jesus's followers. So argues Frederick W. Danker (1920–2012) in this essay that explores the sweeping and inclusive nature of Luke's twin writings. With a thorough and unequaled knowledge of Luke's original language and an impressive understanding of Luke's cultural milieu, Danker offers the reader new insights and a fuller understanding of the Luke-Acts narrative.

Beyond Borders with Saint Luke

by Dr. Frederick W. Danker

80 pages (2018) ISBN: 97817320-48300

Hardback: $16.00

The Challenge for Men: Christian Growth in Spiritual Leadership forces men into action in their present environment and within their personal life situations. The actions have varying degrees, which are different for each man. The challenge for each man to stretch his Christian experience by completing specific actions to expand his relationships with other individuals and his own growth.

by Glenn Daily
Facilitator's Guide
Personal Growth Journal
The Challenge for Men: Christian Growth in Spiritual Leadership
Coming Summer 2025

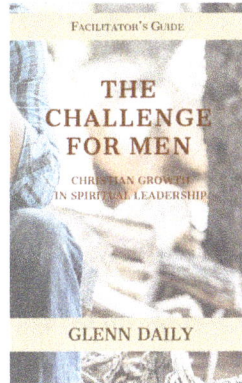

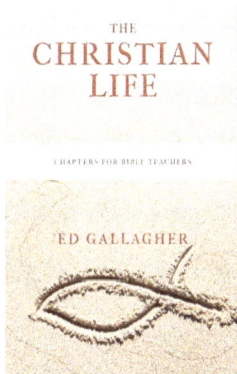

What is the Christian life supposed to look like? What kinds of things ought Christians be doing? This little book—designed as a simple, biblical study for teachers of Bible classes and small groups—focuses on the human response to God's offer of grace. With chapters on the labels applied to Christians in the New Testament, basic elements of the Christian religion, along with the importance of worship, Scripture, the Christian mission, and more, this book will remind Christians of how their lives ought to be structured and challenge them to pursue a more profound engagement with the God who loves them.

The Christian Life: Chapters for Bible Teachers
by Ed Gallagher
102 pages (2021) ISBN: 97810879-64508
Paperback: $10.99
E-book: $9.99

Cruciform Christ is a journey with Jesus through the Gospel of Mark. The Gospel of Mark is broken into fifty-two short chapters, each discussing a major theme, miracle, challenge, or story in the life of Jesus. Each chapter concludes with a series of questions for personal consideration or small group discussion.

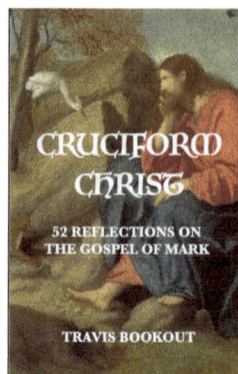

Cruciform Christ: 52 Reflections on the Gospel of Mark

by Travis J. Bookout
350 pages (2022) ISBN: 97819568-11001
Paperback: $22.99
E-book: $15.99

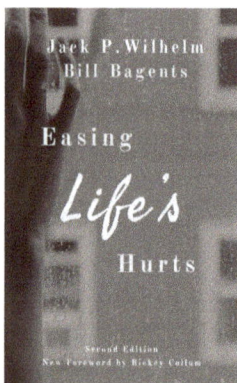

Easing Life's Hurts compassionately encourages readers to choose a biblical perspective toward facing life's bumps, bruises, and disappointments. While optimistic, it makes no claim that all life's hurts can be blocked. God shows amazing grace in using our hurts to shape our souls toward wisdom, kindness, and understanding.

Easing Life's Hurts

by Jack Wilhelm and Bill Bagents
Second edition
220 pages (2020) ISBN: 978817347-66516
Paperback: $12.99
E-book: $9.99

Ecclesiastes: A Document Designed to Disturb offers a fresh, realistic, and engaging interaction with one of Scripture's most enigmatic books. Coy Roper's conversational style invites readers to approach Ecclesiastes from Solomon's often dark perspective. From a temporal perspective, life is amazingly unfair, unpredictable, and uncontrollable. In thirteen chapters, each including probing questions, Roper invites an optimistic exploration of Ecclesiastes.

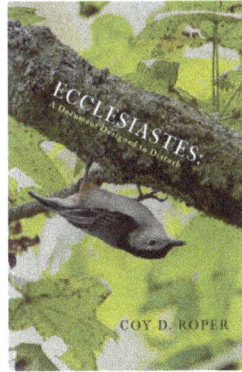

Ecclesiastes: A Document Designed to Disturb
by Coy D. Roper
203 pages (2022) ISBN: 97819568-11230
Paperback: $14.99
E-book: $12.99

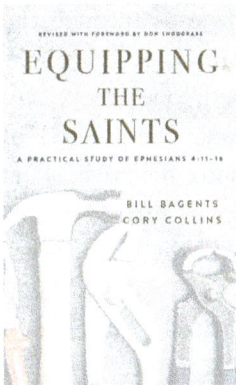

Ephesians 4:11–16 offers instruction and encouragement for all who want to help the church grow, challenging every Christian to grow into more abundant service. *Equipping the Saints* engages this rich text on a real-world level. It invites you to ask, "How can God use me to bless His church?"

Equipping the Saints: A Practical Study of Ephesians 4:11–16
by Bill Bagents and Cory Collins
114 pages (2019) ISBN: 97817320-48355
Paperback: $11.99
E-book: $9.99

Getting My Heart Right With God offers twenty-plus essays on God and ministry written over almost twenty years of teaching and kingdom-work. In four sections, Bagents explores God, Grace, Service, and Leadership. Hundreds of Bible citations invite readers to further study. Essays include "God the Master Servant," "God's Responses to Human Complaints," "Connecting to God," and more.

Getting My Heart Right with God
by Bill Bagents
254 pages (2023)
ISBN: 97819568-11452
Paperback: $15.99
E-book: $13.99

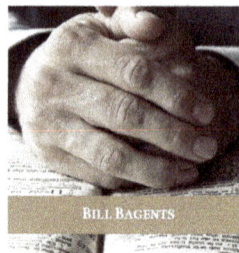

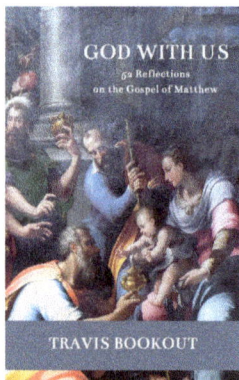

God With Us: 52 Reflections on the Gospel of Matthew is a journey with Jesus through the Gospel of Matthew. It can be read straight through or slowly digested, one week at a time, for a year-long study. The Gospel of Matthew is broken up into fifty-two short chapters each discussing a major theme, teaching, miracle, or story in the life of Jesus. Special attention is given to His divine identity, His role as the authoritative Teacher of Israel, His fulfillment of Scripture, and His kingship over all the earth. Each reflection concludes with a series of questions for personal consideration or small group discussion.

God With Us: 52 Reflections on the Gospel of Matthew
by Travis J. Bookout
287 pages (2024)
ISBN: 97819568-11650
Paperback: $23.99
Ebook: $21.99

The Holy Spirit stays true to its title, offering a detailed discussion of the person, nature, purpose, and work of the Spirit. As those who knew Jack Wilhelm would expect, it is replete with biblical citations and references. Readers can't miss the underlying call to read the Bible, and give honest best effort to understanding the Bible.

The Holy Spirit: A Bible Study Guide
by Jack P. Wilhelm
231 pages (2021)
ISBN: 97810879-39292
Paperback: $12.99
E-book: $9.99

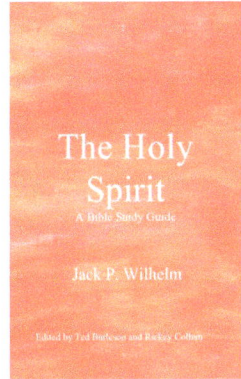

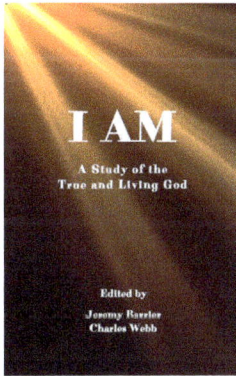

I AM: A Study of the True and Living God presents 15 essays that introduce its reader to the character and greatness of the God of the Bible. Although written in English, it was created primarily to be translated into Hindi to aid evangelism in India. It has also been translated into Lisu for use in Myanmar and adjacent sections of China. Chapters include, "I AM Triune," "I AM Almighty," "I AM Holy," "I AM Truth," and "I AM Love."

I AM: A Study of the True and Living God
edited by Jeremy Barrier and Charles R. Webb
221 pages (2010)
ISBN: 97819568-11377
Paperback: $12.99
E-book: $10.99

Imperative invites thoughtful and creative interaction with the New Testament's most practical and prescriptive book. Berlanga identifies and discusses more than fifty instances where James uses the imperative mood to warn, instruct, command, and motivate believers. It's not a grammar book; rather, *Imperative* employs knowledge of grammar and communication to urge dynamic Christian living. Berlanga's book is as fresh as it is engaging.

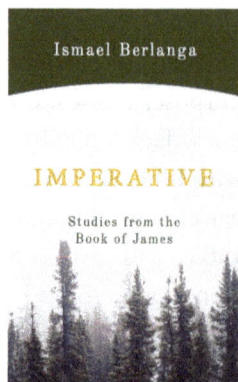

Imperative: Studies from the Book of James
by Ismael Berlanga
412 pages (2022)
ISBN: 97819568-11339
Paperback: $15.99 — E-book: $13.99

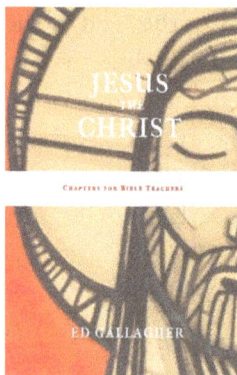

In thirteen brief chapters, Gallagher examines the Old Testament promises of a future king who would rule God's people, and how Jesus both fulfilled these promises while also subverting the expectations of His contemporaries regarding the coming king. Each chapter is organized around a series of questions ideal for promoting discussion in a small group or Bible class.

Jesus the Christ: Chapters for Bible Teachers
by Ed Gallagher
124 pages (2021)
ISBN: 97810879-60425
Paperback: $10.99
E-book: $9.99

Having the depth of a commentary, yet accessible to any Christian, *King of Glory* is filled with practical ways to actualize the call of John's Gospel-to embody the love of God and glorify Christ through acts of service, justice, and self-sacrifice.

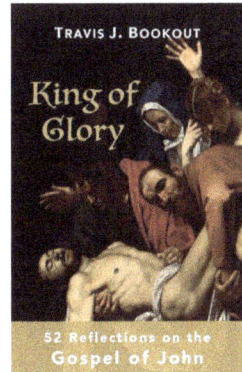

King of Glory: 52 Reflections on the Gospel of John
  by Travis J. Bookout
  260 pages (2021)
  ISBN: 97817347-66554
  Paperback: $14.99
  E-book: $12.99

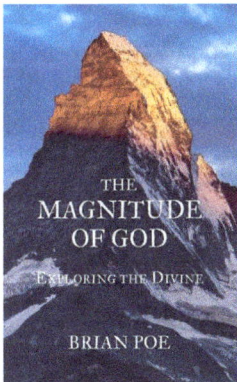

The Magnitude of God: Exploring the Divine offers a fresh and engaging reminder of the unparalleled magnificence of the Almighty. In an age of diminished appreciation for and understanding of God, Brian Poe invites readers to revisit Scripture and remember just how BIG God is. In five sections, Poe explores and extolls God's voice, presence, testimony, awe, and greatness.

The Magnitude of God: Exploring the Divine
  by Brian Poe
  149 pages (2022)
  ISBN: 97819568-11353
  Paperback: $12.99
  E-book: $10.99

This collection of outlines, originally compiled by the respected preacher, teacher, author, and administrator Jack Wilhelm prior to his death in 2016, helps fill that space on the bookshelf by bringing together over fifty outlines from Churches of Christ ministers throughout the United States. Many of these outlines contain widely applicable thoughts and scriptural passages, while others are tailored for use in specific circumstances, such as the death of a young church member or of a congregation's elder.

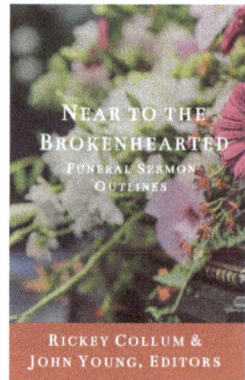

Near to the Brokenhearted: Funeral Sermon Outlines
edited by Rickey Collum and John Young
192 pages (2024) — ISBN: 978-1-956811-91-9
Paperback: $12.99 — Ebook: $10.99

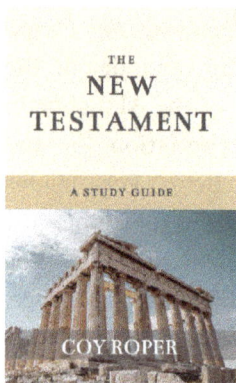

As the late Coy Roper taught Critical Introduction to the New Testament, he improved and expanded the notes he shared with his students. *The New Testament: A Study Guide* is the culmination of those efforts. Chapters include "Scriptures Related to the Inspiration of the New Testament." "Canon of the New Testament," "Textual Criticism of the New Testament" and "Suggestions Regarding Translations." *The New Testament: A Study Guide* offers seasoned insights and connections to numerous essential resources for effectively studying the Christian Bible.

The New Testament: A Study Guide
by Coy D. Roper
260 pages (2024) — ISBN: 97819568-11575
Hardback: $19.99 — E-book: $17.99

As the late Coy Roper taught Critical Introduction to the Old Testament, he improved and expanded the notes he shared with his undergraduate students. *The Old Testament: A Study Guide* is the culmination of those efforts. Chapters include "The Christian View of the Old Testament." "Canon of the Old Testament," "Survey of Approaches to the Study of the Old Testament" and "Preaching from the Old Testament." *The Old Testament: A Study Guide* offers seasoned insights and connections to numerous essential resources for the effective study of the Hebrew Bible.

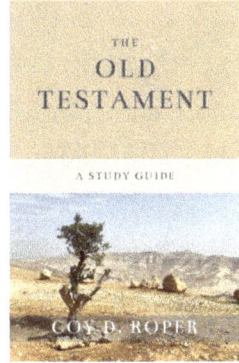

The Old Testament: A Study Guide
by Coy D. Roper
316 pages (2024) — ISBN: 97819568-11537
Hardback: $24.99 — E-book: $22.99

The book is a study guide through the pre-exilic prophets for those seeking to do a deeper study. It is designed to read alongside the prophetic books of the Bible to help make sense of some of the most difficult biblical literature. It offers insightful commentary on key issues and passages as well as seeking to help the reader reflect on the importance of the prophetic message for today. This book goes in chronological order and provides insights into the political and historical backdrop that is vital to understanding the message.

The Pre-Exilic Prophets: A Commentary and Reflection
by Blake Hayes
146 pages (2025) ISBN:
Paperback:
E-book:

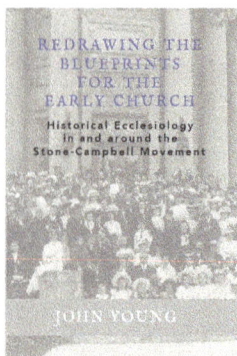

Redrawing the Blueprints reveals that members of the Stone-Campbell (or Restoration) Movement actually participated in a distinctively historical project because their efforts necessarily involved reading sources from and about the past and drawing conclusions about those readings. Through a variety of sources, John Young illustrates that restorationist groups have historically participated in a common pursuit of the early church.

Redrawing the Blueprints for the Early Church: Historical Ecclesiology in and around the Stone-Campbell Movement

by John Young

188 pages (2021) ISBN: 97817374-76678

Hardback: $32.99

E-book: $29.99

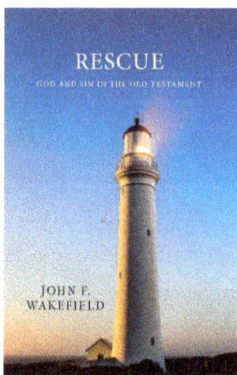

Since creation, God has watched over people. When they needed a rescue from sin in Old Testament times, He alerted them to the spiritual danger. In *Rescue: God and Sin in the Old Testament*, Wakefield analyzes twenty-two cases of rescue (or offered rescue) from sin. Each chapter includes suggested implications for Christians, and questions at the end of each chapter provide opportunities for further study.

Rescue: God and Sin in the Old Testament

by John F. Wakefield

240 pages (2021) ISBN: 97810879-55520

Hardback: $23.99

E-book: $17.99

Revisiting Life's Oases: Soul-Soothing Stories may tell you more about the author than you ever wanted to know. Chances are you'll smile, laugh, and maybe sympathize. You may even cry, wonder, disbelieve, or tell yourself, "Well, that explains a lot." If so, mission accomplished. Stories are gifts from God. If this set of stories encourages you to value and share your own heart with others, may God bless you for blessing them.

Revising Life's Oases: Soul-Soothing Stories
by Bill Bagents
130 pages (2021) ISBN: 97810879-47112
Paperback: $12.99
E-book: $9.99

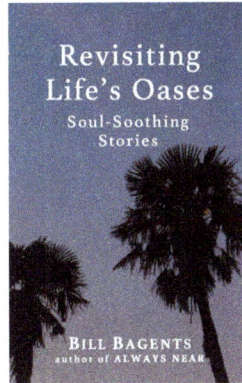

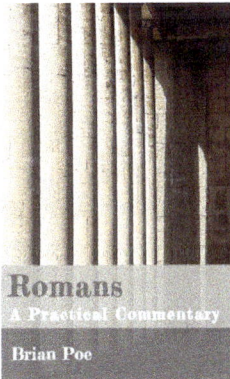

This commentary on the book of Romans is an easy-to-read book on the letter Paul wrote to the church in Rome. In this commentary, Poe goes from chapter to chapter walking through the content and brings a relevant understanding to the text. *Romans: A Practical Commentary* is a perfect balance of depth and simplicity designed for the average person.

Romans: A Practical Commentary
by Brian Poe
206 pages (2023) ISBN: 97819568-11216

Paperback: $14.99
E-book: $12.99

Cover
Coming
Soon

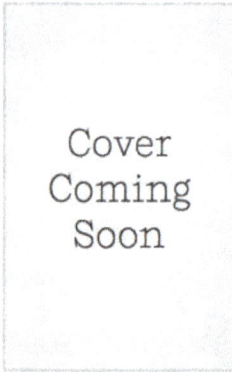

When an author is diving into human behavior, and then placing alongside considerations of religious faith and practice, there will inevitably be plenty of serious stuff for the reader. But church history can also be fun. The history of the Stone-Campbell Movement contains no shortage of surprising plot twists, bizarre asides, unexpected ties to political developments, celebrity sightings, and even some good old-fashioned rumor-mongering. The author hopes you'll have fun reading about these kinds of things.

Silly Songs, Surprising Stories, and Supreme Court Justices: The Wild Fun-tier of Stone-Campbell Movement History

by John Young
134 pages (2025) ISBN: 97819568-11995
Paperback: $15.99 E-book: 13.99

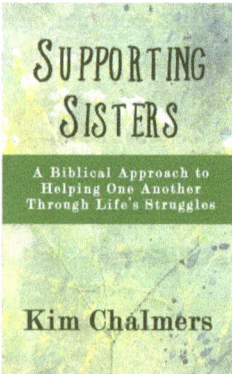

SUPPORTING
SISTERS

A Biblical Approach to
Helping One Another
Through Life's Struggles

Kim Chalmers

Kim Chalmers's book, *Supporting Sisters: A Biblical Approach to Helping One Another Through Life's Struggles*, is a foundational resource for Christian ladies who want to provide counsel, support, and encouragement for their sisters in Christ. Chalmers writes with passion and practicality, linking key concepts of helping to biblical principles and examples. *Supporting Sisters* equips and encourages spiritual women to bless their peers with the love and wisdom of the Lord.

Supporting Sisters: A Biblical Approach to Helping One Another Through Life's Struggles.

by Kim Chalmers
160 pages (2025) ISBN: Forthcoming
Paperback: $16.99 E-book: $14.99

According to Coy Roper, Christians who do their best to obey the Bible are, under ordinary circumstances, more likely to prosper than they would if they were not faithful Christians. *That All May Go Well* is a thoughtful examination of the complexities that underlie the question— "Why do Christians prosper?" Roper presents a balanced theology of prosperity by tackling poverty and financial insecurity, as well as the dangers of materialism.

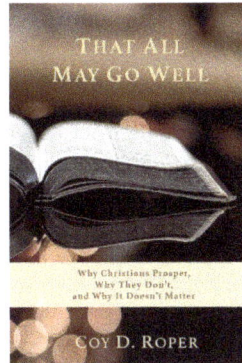

That All May Go Well: Why Christians Prosper, Why They Don't, and Why It Doesn't Matter
by Coy D. Roper
154 pages (2020)
ISBN: 97817320-48379
Paperback: $8.99

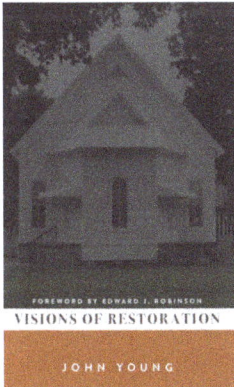

In *Visions of Restoration*, historian John Young provides a highly readable, easily accessible overview of the history of Churches of Christ stretching from the early nineteenth century to the early twenty-first century. The target audience is primarily members of Churches of Christ who are new to the study of their fellowship's history. Also, at a length of thirteen short chapters, it is designed to be used in Sunday-school type settings.

Visions of Restoration: The History of Churches of Christ
by John Young
111 pages (2019)
ISBN: 97817320-48348
Paperback: $12.99
E-book: $9.99

Because He loves us, God calls us to hear Him well. Because we love Him, we must answer that call. Thus, *Welcoming God's Word*—a series of invitations to hear God well and to let Him help us live in His grace. Enjoy the adventure.

Welcoming God's Word: Reading with Head and Heart

by Bill Bagents
299 pages (2021)
ISBN: 97810879-39315
Paperback: $14.99
E-book: $10.99

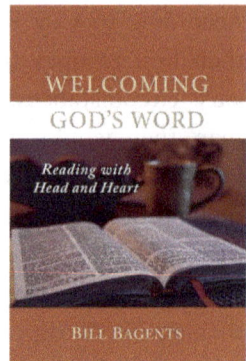

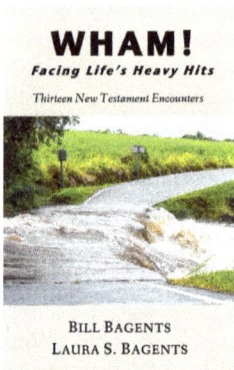

Because life includes major blows to heart, head, health, faith, finances, and relationships, *WHAM! Facing Life's Heavy Hits: Thirteen New Testament Encounters* offers a fresh and focused look at thirteen familiar stories and lives. This book promotes pervasive interaction with Scripture that honors God and welcomes His daily help. Each chapter includes discussion questions appropriate for either individual or group use.

WHAM! Facing Life's Heavy Hits: Thirteen New Testament Encounters

By Bill Bagents and Laura S. Bagents
115 pages (2022)
ISBN: 97819568-11292
Paperback: $10.99
E-book: $9.99

Because life includes major blows to heart, head, health, faith, finances, and relationships, *WHAM! Facing Life's Heavy Hits* offers a fresh and focused look at thirteen familiar Old Testament stories. This book promotes pervasive interaction with Scripture that honors God and welcomes His daily help. Each chapter includes discussion questions appropriate for either individual or group use.

WHAM! Facing Life's Heavy Hits: Thirteen Old Testament Encounters

    by Bill Bagents and Laura S. Bagents

    130 pages (2022)

    ISBN: 97819568-11254

    Paperback: $10.99

    E-book: $9.99

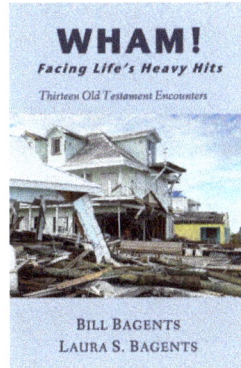

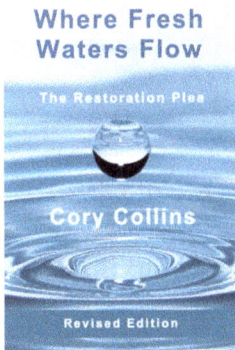

Water at its clearest, purest, and healthiest is always found at the source. One who has tasted that water treasures it highly and returns to it often, resisting and refusing any possible contamination. *Where Fresh Waters Flow: the Restoration Plea* challenges the reader to revisit the faith, teaching, and practice authorized for the first-century church. It calls the reader to drink deeply from God's spring and to draw others to the New Testament's Christ-centered, life-giving, thirst-quenching message.

Where Fresh Waters Flow Revised edition

    by Cory Collins

    194 pages (2025)

    ISBN: 97819568-11827

    Paperback $15.99 — Ebook $13.99

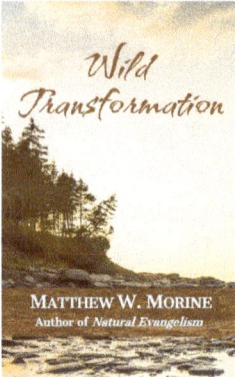

Wild Transformation flows from the heart of Matthew Morine's personal walk with God. From painfully honest descriptions of struggle to soaring stories of victory, it's a hope-infusing book. Jesus walks with us through the process of sanctification. When we're at our best—and sometimes even at our worst, we can choose to see His grace in every step. It's an engaging book that merits serious reading. Each of the thirteen chapters includes discussion questions for either individual or group exploration.

Wild Transformation
by Matthew W. Morine
142 pages (2023)
ISBN: 97819568I-10438
Paperback: $12.99 E-book: $10.99

Wisdom from a Life in Ministry is a collection of brief essays from beloved minister Bob Plunket. Plunket's wry humor and perceptive observation of human nature invite readers back to a somewhat distant—and simpler— time. This book exhibits the power of respectful, biblical thinking as it pleasantly promotes godly values that build strong families, churches, and communities.

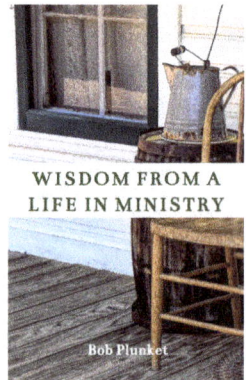

Wisdom from a Life in Ministry
by Bob Plunket
170 pages (2023)
ISBN: 97819568-11513
Paperback: $10.99
E-book: $9.99

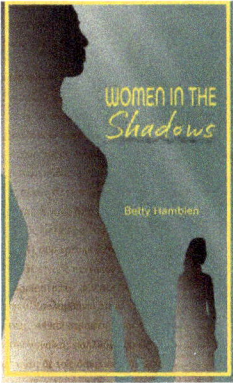

Women in the Shadows faithfully and creatively explores the biblical stories of twelve unnamed women. Creatively, Dr. Hamblen imagines the self-talk and struggles of each lady. Faithfully, she shares timeless and priceless truths from each account. Each chapter concludes with questions well worth pondering. *Women in the Shadows* offers a fresh and engaging approach to texts—and people—who have been woefully neglected in both personal study and Bible classes.

Women in the Shadows
by Betty Hamblen
145 pages (2022)
ISBN: 97819568-11315
Paperback: $12.99
E-book: $10.99

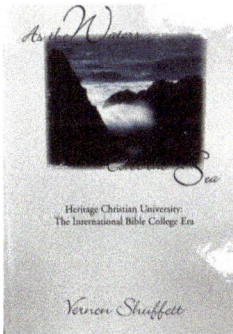

Written by Vice-President Vernon Shuffett, *As the Waters Cover the Sea* is a history of Heritage Christian University between 1971 and 2000 when the institution was named International Bible College. Shuffett delivers a distinct and detailed history due to his accounting background which allows the reader to learn fascinating stories and little-known bits of trivia.

As the Waters Cover the Sea

by Vernon Shuffett
198 pages (2002)
Hardback $10.00

Forthcoming

Confidence in Your Obedience: Favorite Passages from the Sermon on the Mount
    Onesimus Bible Study Series Summer 2025

The Bond of Peace: The Seven Ones from Ephesians 4
    Berean Study Series Spring 2026

Joy and Comfort: Favorite Psalms
    Onesimus Bible Study Series Summar 2026

Someone Is Coming
    Berean Study Series (Spring 2027)

Someone Is Here
    Berean Study Series (Spring 2028)

Someone Is Coming Again
Berean Study Series (2029)

Title Index

Author Index

Ordering Information

Ways to Order

•Online at **www.hcu.edu/publications**
  •Email **press@hcu.edu**
  •Use the **order form** from the **back of this catalog** and mail it to:

- Heritage Christian University Press
- P.O. Box HCU
- Florence, AL35630

Pricing
•9.5% sales tax is added to all orders, except congregations and other tax-exempt organizations
•Payment is due at the time of purchase
•40% discount is available on orders of ten (10) or more books (same or mixed titles).
•Shipping is an additional charge.

Shipping

- •1-5 copies—$4.99
- •6-10 copies—$8.99
- •11-25 copies—$12.99
- •26-50 copies—$19.99
- •51+ copies—$25.99

Need Assistance?

press@hcu.edu

To see the full catalog of Heritage Christian University Press and its imprint, Cypress Publications, visit
www.hcu.edu/publications

Order Form

Order Information   *Date:* _____

Name/Organization_____
Shipping/Delivery Address_____
_____
P.O. Box # (if applicable)_____
Phone Number_____

Title's Item # (last 5 digits of ISBN)	*Quantity*	*Price per Book*	*Subtotal for Each Title*
Item(s) Subtotal			
40% discount (IF applicable)			
Subtotal			
9.5% Sales Tax			
Shipping/Delivery Charge			
Grand Total			

Please tear this page from the catalog and mail it to:

Heritage Christian University Press
P.O. Box HCU
Florence, AL 35630

www.ingramcontent.com/pod-product-compliance
Lightning Source LLC
Chambersburg PA
CBHW060256030426
42335CB00014B/1730